POCKET I

Leyland

Jack Iddon (1902-1946), Leyland and Lancashire cricketer.

POCKET IMAGES

Leyland

DAVID HUNT & WILLIAM WARING

in association with
SOUTH RIBBLE MUSEUM AND EXHIBITION CENTRE
& THE LEYLAND HISTORICAL SOCIETY

Directors leaving a meeting during the great Leyland Motors financial crisis of the early 1920s. Not for the last time in the twentieth century, a period of painful re-adjustment was to form the basis of the company's recovery and future prosperity.

First published in 1995
This new pocket edition 2006
Images unchanged from first edition

Reprinted in 2011 by
The History Press
The Mill, Brimscombe Port,
Stroud, Gloucestershire, GL5 2QG
www.thehistorypress.co.uk

British Library Cataloguing in Publication Data.
A catalogue record for this book is available from the British Library.

ISBN 978-1-84588-288-4

Printed in Malta

Contents

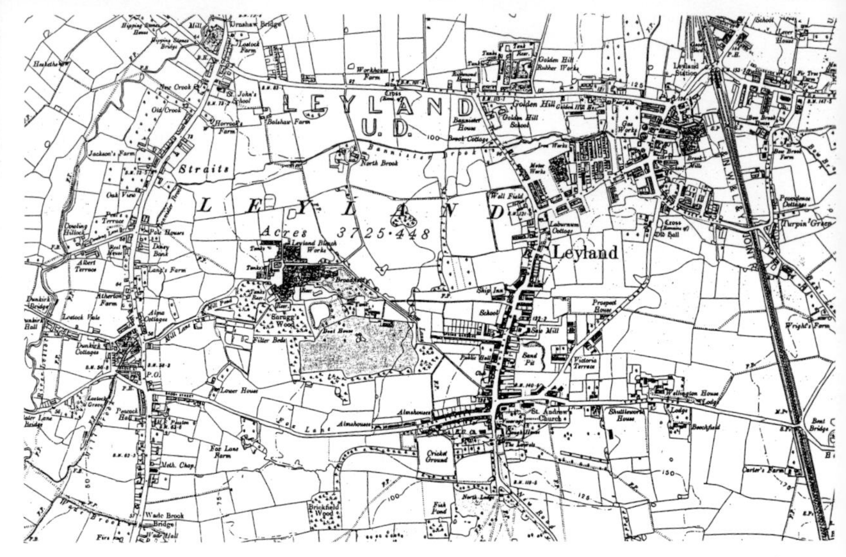

Leyland in 1908. Leyland Library possesses a full set of the series of Ordnance Survey maps of the Borough of South Ribble produced at various scales from the 1840s onwards.

Introduction

Visiting Leyland in the 1870s, Anthony Hewitson was impressed by the village's pastoral beauty. Indeed he was willing to back Leylanders 'against all the tribes of the earth' when it came to gardening. The Revd T.R. Baldwin, 'a beefy, condensed, strong-lunged gentleman', maintained the Baldwin dynasty in the office of vicar, and the Faringtons of Worden were still the power in the land as they had been for centuries. Among the rich farmlands of the west he encountered the rural community along the moss-side, 'a flat peaty, moderately-civilised part of the country'. Yet the Preston journalist also noted the signs of incipient change in this evocative landscape, 'Leyland is a busy village, and an additional impetus is given to its commercial life by sundry adjoining manufactures'; for along Chapel Brow and Golden Hill he observed 'Gas, cotton, steam, railway wagons and drink, five of the most certain coinmaking articles known'. In fact Leyland stood on the verge of the most exciting period of its history, as it entered a second industrial revolution based on the rubber and motor vehicle industries.

As early as the 1780s Leyland handloom weavers were exporting cloth, to be made up into slave's clothing, to the West Indian colonies, and bleaching was established at Northbrook and Shruggs. The textile sector continued to be an important local employer well beyond 1951, when this series of photographs broadly ends. A century later, with the establishment of the rubber industry and the early stirrings of what was to become Leyland Motors, the growing town began to emerge as one of the great powerhouses of British industry – a process that was to be virtually complete within a single lifetime. Centred close to the railway, on Golden Hill Lane and Hough Lane, the factories formed an entirely new nucleus lying to the north of the Cross, and whose population came to work and went home each day. Around the Cross lay the old village core framed within its medieval Townfields. A short walk down Worden Lane led to yet another Leyland, to Worden Park, the closed and private prerogative of the Faringtons. At its centre Worden Hall was a treasury of antiques and paintings, set amidst classical pleasure grounds which had their origins in the eighteenth century.

This collection of photographs traces the impact on the local community and the landscape, of enormous and sustained social change which reached its peak in the first half of the twentieth century. It was produced by South Ribble Museum and Exhibition Centre and the Leyland Historical Society as a contribution to the centenary celebrations of 'Leyland Motors', and as a means of bringing the Borough's collection of photographs to a wider public. In most cases it has not been possible to date photographs accurately. Most date from the early years of the twentieth century when there was clearly a considerable market for postcards. We are accordingly indebted to the town's small group of professional photographers, particularly to Luke Collinge, Robert Butcher, and later Harry Wade and Francis Turner. As far as possible the authors have acknowledged the donors of photographs, but apologise for any omissions. In Leyland the Museum and Exhibition Centre, the Lancashire County Library, and the British Commercial Vehicle Museum, actively collect photographs, and will be pleased to advise on their conservation. All opinions expressed in the book are solely the responsibility of the authors.

History books should reveal as much about the present as the past, and the scale of change since 1951 is quite staggering. Enormous chunks of the townscape have been almost surgically removed. Although few will doubt the wisdom of relocating the enormous motorworks from Hough Lane to the great assembly hall at Farington, the demolition and subsequent dereliction of Western Towngate (whose buildings are well illustrated here), will be utterly incomprehensible to many. Yet much of the heritage of the first fifty years of the twentieth century is still apparent at the close of the second. Leyland Trucks have emerged very successfully from the wreck of British Leyland and the world is still keen to buy their vehicles, Worden Park is open to all and in the safe custodianship of the Borough Council, and Leylanders can still hold their own against all-comers when it comes to gardening.

One

A Sense of Community

Leyland Cross c.1900. The Rev. Leyland Baldwin leads the hymn singing, probably at the conclusion of the Whitsuntide walk. Although its precise origins and age are uncertain, the cross stands in the centre of the ancient village.

St Andrew's parish church, *c*.1905. Leyland's parish church, and its grounds, was a popular venue for visitors in the early years of the century.

The Vicar's Fields, *c*.1900. Anthony Hewitson wrote of Leyland in the 1870s, 'It stands in a pleasant place, is surrounded on all hands by a unique picture of pastoral beauty – by flowers and fruitful flocks, by blooming orchards and smiling homesteads, by grand old trees and fertile lands'.

The Revd Octavius De Leyland Baldwin, c.1900. Vicar 1891-1911, Leyland Baldwin was a social visionary well ahead of his time. His curate wrote of him, 'I believe he was ever thinking, not of himself, or indeed merely of the present, but of the future, and of posterity. He wanted Leyland to be up-to-date, in sanitation, in education, in cleanliness and in all things which promote the health and happiness of the people at large'.

The Grandstand, May Festival ground, *c*.1905. Leyland Baldwin in earnest conversation with Lord Balcarres.

The May Festival procession 1912. The Morris Men pass along Towngate.

Mowing the churchyard, c.1910.

The church-bells, taken down for re-casting in 1928.

The funeral of Leyland Baldwin, 1913. Leyland Baldwin's death brought to an end the line of Baldwin vicars stretching back over 165 years through seven generations.

St James's church, Moss-side, 1900. Built as a memorial to James Nowell Farington (1813-48), the last in the male line of the Faringtons of Worden, by his widow. Their marriage the year before his death had been cause for much local celebration.

St James's Sunday School procession, c.1900.

St Ambrose's church, Moss Lane, 1900. Built in 1885, the tower was added in 1891, by the Rev. T.R.Baldwin in memory of his wife Elizabeth.

St Ambrose's church, Moss Lane, *c.*1905. Moss Lane originated as the trackway used by people from Clayton to cut peat on Farington Moss. Note the high quality housing, which was to become the hallmark of twentieth century life in Leyland.

St John's school, Earnshaw Bridge, *c*.1920.

The United Reformed church, Hough Lane, *c*.1905. Opened for worship in 1877, the church and the adjacent houses were designed by the local architect David Grant.

The interior of St Mary's RC church, Worden Lane, 1905.

The opening of St Mary's school, 1932. When Balshaw's Grammar School moved to new premises on Church Road in 1931, their Golden Hill school was bought by Fr. Anselm Parker, parish priest, in March 1932.

The RC Whit procession, passing Leyland Cross, early 1930s. The clergy are, left to right: Fr. Rogerson, Fr. Anselm Parker and Fr. Leo Parker.

The Methodists' Whitsuntide procession, 1931. Inspector Ripley leads the walk as it approaches Leyland Cross.

The Methodist chapel, Chapel Brow, *c*.1900.

The Primitive Methodist chapel, Leyland Lane, *c*.1910.

The Primitive Methodist chapel, Leyland Lane, c.1895. Newly completed, and standing in open fields, the church had been opened in 1893 at a cost of £1,028. It duly held its 'New Century' celebrations in 1993.

The Methodist church, Turpin Green Lane, c.1905.

Leyland Cross. The visit of Edward, Prince of Wales to Leyland in 1921. Four ex-servicemen were presented to the prince. R. Kirby is hidden by the man in the foreground, the others are, left to right: Dick Berry, Fred Marsden and Charles Porter.

The coronation arch, Towngate, looking south, 1911. Leyland's extensive church-based community groups, thriving in the town's general air of prosperity and confidence in the years before the Great War, could mobilise considerable resources. A point well made by the extravagant decorations for the coronation of King George V in 1911.

The coronation arch, looking north, 1911.

A coronation banner beside the Queen's Hotel, at the junction of Chapel Brow and Golden Hill Lane, the industrial hub of Leyland by 1911.

Decorations along Chapel Brow, 1911.

Two

A New Industrial Society

The Water Street step-houses, 1934. Handloom weaving in such purpose built cottages, was a conspicuous feature of Leyland's first industrial revolution in the early years of the nineteenth century. These houses consisted of simple two storey dwellings built over semi-subterranean loomshops. A similar design can be seen in the 1790 extension to the Old Grammar School.

The Union Street step-houses, *c*.1909. Built by the Union Street Building Society from 1802, the row occupies one of the medieval field-strips. Funded largely by the local beer trade, the houses are among the finest surviving examples of their type.

The Bradshaw Street step-houses, *c*.1900. Handloom weaving declined markedly during the 1840s, but some weaving seems to have continued in Bradshaw Street for another 20 years. In the 1930s Union Street became a part of Fox Lane, and Bradshaw Street became Spring Gardens.

John Stanning's Broadfield bleach and dye works, 1935. Bleaching was well established in Leyland by the 1780s. John Stanning and Son took over the Shruggs works in 1871, and the firm was to remain a major employer until the closure of the works in the late 1960s.

The packing room at Stannings, *c*.1930.

Broadfield House, Cow Lane, *c*.1905. A suitable residence for one of the town's leading citizens. John Stanning revived Leyland cricket club, and purchased the Old Grammar School for use as a parish hall-thus ensuring the building's survival when the school closed in 1874. An extremely able business man, he was the first chairman of the Bleachers Association, the great cartel of British finishing firms. Broadfield House was built by Stanning alongside the works, and a part of the site is now occupied by the modern catholic church.

Earnshaw Bridge Mill, *c*.1910. By the 1850s local 'manufacturers' had established two spinning and weaving mills along Leyland Lane, forming distinct hamlets at Earnshaw Bridge and Seven Stars. A notable feature of Mr.Pilkington's mill is its superb (and recently restored) engine house.

Farington Mill, c.1935. Built alongside the Preston-Wigan railway in the 1830s, Bashall and Boardman's enormous mill was one of the most profitable in the country. Around it was developed the planned village of modern Farington. The mill boasted one of the tallest and most elegant chimneys at 75 yards, and had its own railway sidings. Rioting Chartists knocked out the boiler plugs in 1842, the hands were locked out by their masters in 1854, the mill was closed for a long period during the Cotton Famine, was burnt down in 1867 and damaged by exploding ammunition in 1942, but survived all these trials to weave out only in the late 1960s.

The interior of Mount Pleasant Mill, c.1910. Leyland's textile industry stood up very well to the trade's troubles of the early twentieth century. In 1939 Andrew Berry and Sons Mount Pleasant mill was operating 1,113 looms, with a further 771 at John Pilkington's Earnshaw Bridge mill. Keith Berry, third from left above, was the founder's grandson.

Brook Mill from Hough Lane, c.1910. Opened by Reade and Wall in the 1870s, Brook Mill was the largest of Leyland's cotton mills.

A weaver in Brook Mill, 1925. Part of a set of photographs produced by the *Daily Mail* in 1925, and now preserved in the South Ribble local history collection.

The Brook Mill tableau, Festival of Britain celebrations, 1951. Brook Mill was one of the last surviving cotton mills in the greater Preston weaving area, when its closure was announced in 1967.

Staff of the Leyland and Birmingham Rubber Company, *c.*1900.

The scene after 'Th' owd rubbber fire' of 1913.

The Leyland and Birmingham Rubber Company, Golden Hill Lane, c.1935. Leyland's second industrial revolution began in the 1870s. By 1873 James Quin was established in Golden Hill Lane, a trackway to the moss, as a maker of waterproof cloths. The introduction of rubber led to great progress with the formation of the Leyland Rubber Co., which in 1898 amalgamated with the Birmingham Rubber Co. Leyland was an early leader in the field, and by the 1920s was host to a number of rubber manufacturers. Ultimately both the L & B, and Wood-Milne became important constituents of BTR Industries, one of Britain's most successful conglomerates, employing 120,000 people in over 100 countries.

The Ajax Rubber Works, *c*.1910. Whitehead and Roberts Ltd, 'Manufacturers of the famous Wood-Milne rubber heels', claimed to be the first in the world to apply rubber to footwear. All sorts of applications of rubber to everyday use were tried, and at one time Leyland could boast a rubber road, hazardous in wet weather.

The L & B Firebrigade with the company's patent hoses well to the fore, 1880. Back row, left to right: W.Rigby, J.Wilding, T.Holt, M.Potter, T.Lancaster, J.Robinson, J.Iddon (Captain). Front row: -?-, E.Kershaw, R.Caunce, G.Bond, W.Sharp, S.Woods, R.Rose, J.E.Baxter (Manager).

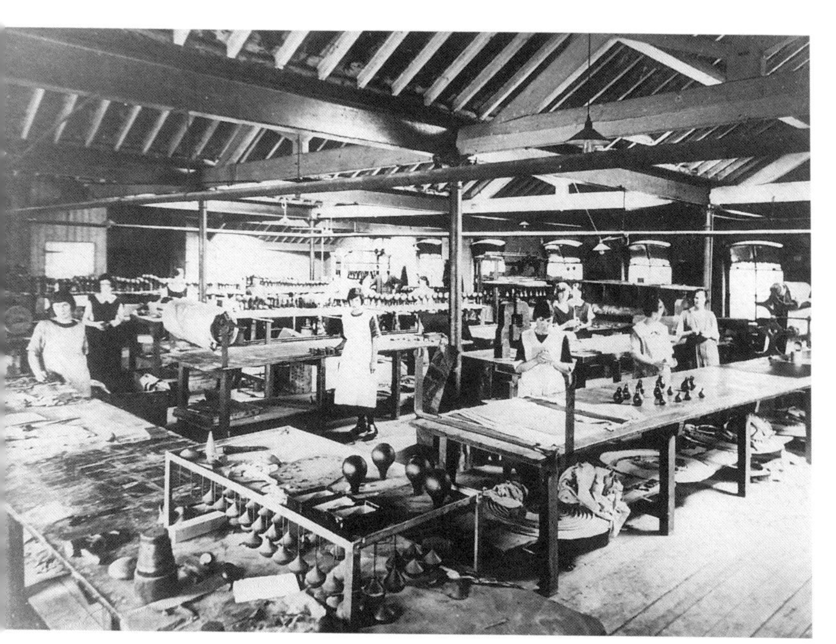

Women at work in the bulb department.

Flexible hoses for the emerging oil industry, c.1905.

The hot water bottle department, c.1920. Leyland's rubber industry employed large numbers of women, particularly during the first world war.

An L & B procession float, c.1920.

Panorama of L & B, BTR and Iddon Brothers, c.1949. A good impression of the concentration of the rubber and related industries along Golden Hill Lane. Taken from the roof of Leyland Motors canteen, looking down Meadow Street and Quin Street, with Hough Lane and the Congregational church in the foreground. Note the camouflaged chimney to the left of the church.

Above: The Leyland Paint and Varnish Company, *c.*1955. In 1922 Mr Fred Jones established what was to become Leyland Paints. Expansion was rapid, and by 1939 the firm had developed a considerable market share and distribution network. In the space of fifty years Leyland had thus given its name to three leaders in different industries, to Leyland Paints, the Leyland and Birmingham Rubber Co., and Leyland Motors, whilst still retaining a strong base in textile manufacturing and processing. These were to be the basis of the towns remarkable progress in the first half of the twentieth century.

Opposite above: Paint mixing, *c.*1955.

Opposite below: The roller mill section at Leyland Paints, *c.*1955.

07752

Leyland paints ready for despatch, c.1955.

The Leyland Paints tableau on a Leyland Motors 'Comet', Festival of Britain, 1951.

Three

Leyland Motors and World Renown

Humble origins; the Sumner smithy in Water Street, *c*.1905.

The Leyland Motors factories, *c*.1955. From the bottom up: the athletic grounds, South Works, (Hough Lane), North Works, (Golden Hill Lane), the Farington Works, and Spurrier Works. The enormous assembly plant of Leyland Trucks has since been built beyond Spurrier Works. During the 1880s James Sumner was able to experiment in the Water Street smithy with early and primitive powered vehicles. These efforts culminated in the formation of James Sumner Ltd, and in 1896 the Lancashire Steam Motor Co was formed with the financial backing of Henry Spurrier the first, and the firm moved to Herbert Street. As early as 1905 the Rev Marshall, Leyland Baldwin's curate, could write with evident satisfaction, 'Leyland has the proud distinction of having invented the first steam lawnmower: Mr. James Sumner being the inventor. This gentleman is now a managing director and also a partner in the Lancashire Steam Motor Co. Ltd., whose extensive works are at Leyland'.

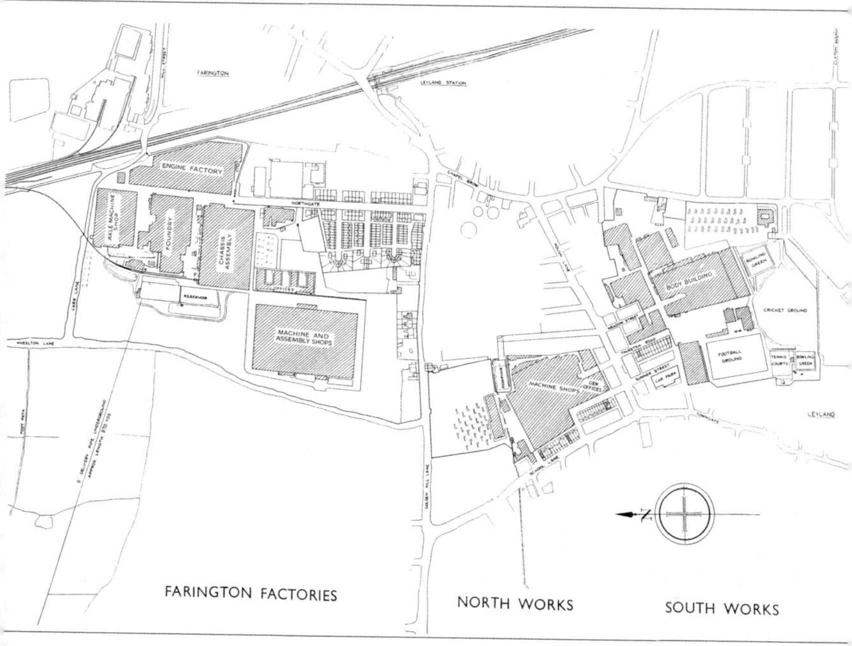

The map of the works in the late 1950s. The enormous impact of the works on the townscape is clear. No less remarkable than the rapid development of the works on Hough Lane in the years up to 1930, was to be their even more rapid removal in the 1980s, and the relocation of the enterprise at an entirely new site in Farington.

The interior of the smithy, *c*.1906. Some idea of the resources available to James Sumner can be gained from this view of the workshop when it was subsequently occupied by George Damp and Sons. Left to right: John Damp, Edward Damp, George Damp, -?-, W.Buck.

Steam wagons in School Lane, *c*.1910. Large numbers of steam wagons were produced, many of which were found to be doing good service twenty five years later. In 1904 the first petrol vehicle left the works, and the first petrol driven bus was supplied to the London and Suburban Omnibus Co. the following year.

The employees of the Lancashire Steam Wagon Co., *c*.1900. In 1903 the firm was re-formed with a share capital of £50,000, adopting the name Leyland Motors in 1907. Seven years later Leyland Motors (1914) had a share capital of £400,000, employed 1,500 people, and had completed over 2,000 petrol driven vehicles in addition to a large number of steamers. Above left is James Sumner, with Henry Spurrier (the second), second right.

Wartime production, 1915. The two wars were to be important factors in the growth of the firm. The War Office placed 'colossal' orders totalling eighty eight vehicles in 1912-3, but during the first war over 6,000 vehicles were produced.

A convoy of Leylands at Pincock, en route for London. Despite buying back 4,000 government vehicles after the war, over expansion almost caused the firm to founder in the early 1920s.

John Godfrey Parry Thomas (1885-1927), c.1924. Thomas was chief engineer at Leyland 1917-23. Sir Henry Spurrier wrote of him, 'I remember him as a Welshman with a dynamic and arresting personality, intolerant, of course, as are all good engineers, probably the most brilliant inventor of his day, and kind and generous, with a helping hand for anyone in need'.

A Straight-Eight chassis, at the main entrance in Northcote Street, 1921. Thomas, with his assistant 'Oozalong' Railton, stated the intention 'to produce the most perfect car it is possible to design and manufacture'. Indeed 'the only car that we consider as a sparring partner to the Leyland Eight is the Rolls-Royce'. In 1920 the chassis alone was priced at £2,500, and the commercial crisis killed off the venture. Only fourteen cars were built; two were sold to the Maharajah of Patiala, and Michael Collins bought one. In 1924 Thomas set a new world land speed record in a Leyland car, 129.73MPH. He was killed in a subsequent car, 'Babs', on Pendine Sands in February 1927, trying to wrest the record from Malcom Campbell's 'Bluebird'.

A Leyland Straight-Eight, Northcote Street. 1921. Parry Thomas, wearing a trilby is standing fourth from left, Newton Iddon is standing seventh from left.

Newton Iddon at the wheel of the restored Straight-Eight, Worden Lane, 1964. In the late 1950s a surviving car was found in a London garage, purchased by Sir Henry Spurrier, and restored at Leyland under the supervision of Newton Iddon, who had been one of Thomas's apprentices.

A 'P-type' flat platform lorry, c.1920. As early as 1910 the Preston firm of Viney's had purchased an impressive fleet of Leyland steam wagons. The Ribble Bus Company, first established in Gregson Lane, Higher Walton, was also to be an important local customer.

The directors and senior management, c.1925. A sports day on the grounds established behind the South Works. Back row, left to right: Mr Toulmin, Henry Spurrier (the second), -?- , Mr Liardet, Mr Phillips-Conn, Mr Elkington, Mr Hoskins, Mr Davies, Mr Wilde. Front Row, Mr Davenport, Mr Brown, Mr Skipper, Mr Pilkington, Mr Langtree, Mr Lockwood. Mr Liardet was 'put in by the bank' to rescue the firm, and 'stayed on', to be General Manager from 1923.

Managers, foremen, and superintendants outside the new 'Leyland Motors Sports and Athletic Club', 1921. Back row, left to right:, Jimmy Barker, Charlie Lockwood, Jack Brierley, Bert Rimmer, Jim Holden, Harry Waring, Jim Sanderson, Jim Mc Man, Arthur Leyland. Middle row, Walter Laithwaite, Bill Mather, Walter Schofield, -?-, Bill Wilcox, -?-, T.Helme, Alf Holden, Jim Sanderson, -?-, -?-, Alan Copley, Ralph Arrowsmith. Front row: Frank Pye, Tom Clarkson, Sam Sutton, Bob Clayton, Bill Lowe (Works Manager), Bill Sumner, John Sumner, Percy Major, Evelyn Buckley, Dick Astin, Charlie Shepherd.

A Leyland 'Tiger' in John Fishwick's livery, c.1935. Produced 1927-42, this was one of a number of very successful and innovative designs, well ahead of its rivals. Great emphasis was placed on advertising, 'You can't tread on the tail of a Tiger!'.

A Leyland six wheeled trolleybus, c.1938. London Transport was the largest operator of these vehicles with over 1,800, half of them Leylands. Using cheap municipal current the trollybus was a natural development for bus manufacturers.

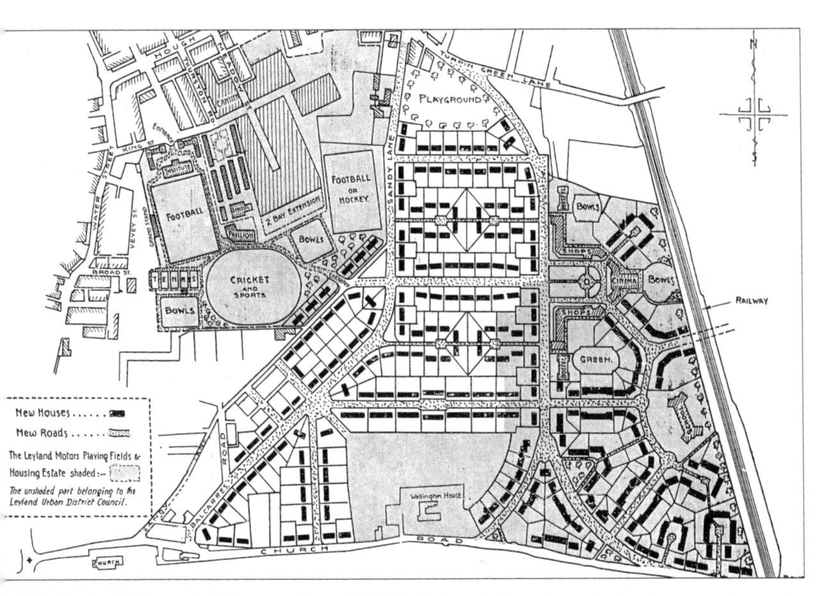

The Leyland Motors Ltd Housing Plan, 1919-20. Although the scheme had to be somewhat curtailed, a large part of the planned development did take place, forming Leyland's 'garden suburb' between Sandy Lane and the railway in the 1930s.

A contrast; houses clustered around the Hough Lane works, *c*.1935. The Gas Works and Brook Mill, at the east end of Hough Lane.

Left: Gear cutting machines, *c*.1945. An important feature of wartime production was the extended employment of women, whose numbers rose from less than 500 in 1939, to almost 3,000 by the peak of production in 1944.

Below: A Centaur Tank, undergoing tests, 1942. Production again soared during the war as the firm became a specialist tank producer.

The drawing office, 1945.

The Farington foundry, c.1935. The foundry was clearly a key target of enemy action: 'The steel foundry has a total area of 7,000 square yards, having three bays, 350' long by 60' wide. It has a capacity for dealing with 130 tons of electric steel per week, large quantities of which are supplied to the Admiralty and leading ship-building and engineering firms throughout the British Isles'.

The Farington foundry, *c*.1945. One of the electric arc steel melting furnaces at Farington. Originally built in the first war, they were pushed into service again during the second as the works were operated day and night to meet production targets. Watching the proceedings is metallurgist Bert Humble.

The BX factory at Farington, 1945. A blend of wartime and civilian vehicles on the assembly line at the end of the war.

Assembling 'Comet' trucks in the BX factory at Farington, 1950.

Chassis assembly in the BX factory, Farington, 1950s. The chain driven assembly track was the first of its kind in Europe.

Into the post-war era with confidence; the entrance to the North Works, mid-1960s.

Four

North of Leyland Cross: Vanished Towngate

Towngate, 1960. The view of much of the old village centre seen from the top of Fox Lane, just before the developers moved in. A Fishwick's double-decker, service 111, is on its way to Preston.

Left: Leyland village cross and pump. Pre-1887. Leyland Baldwin was informed in 1901, that 'Since Leyland was a coming place, an improvement of which it stood in need, was the removal of the village cross, and the erection of an incandescent lamp in its stead, flanked on either side by a public urinal'!

Below: Towngate looking north, c.1910. A fine view of the three storey building on the corner of Cow Lane. On the right is John Heaton's ironmongers, a shop that sold everything. Note the sign above the door for 'Pratt's Motor Oil'. In the days before petrol stations petrol was sold from shops such as this.

Leyland Cross and Towngate, 1950. From the early 1960s the (to date) ill-fated schemes to redevelop western Towngate have resulted only in the wholesale removal of this historic landscape. Only the cross survives to survey the wilderness.

Leyland Cross and Jubilee fountain, c.1905. For the 1887 Jubilee the lights were removed, and the fountain was erected.

Towngate shops, 1950. Nick Blackledge (left), road-sweeper for the LUDC, and Harry Waring, tailor and outfitter, outside 41 and 43 Towngate. Mr Martin, manager of the Lancashire Electric Power Co.'s shop, can be seen on the extreme left. North End's away form was clearly causing concern, in this scene caught by local photographer Francis Turner.

Towngate decorated for the coronation of George V, 1911. The three storey house is a fine example of a local eighteenth-century type of which there were several examples in Leyland. The downstairs front rooms were converted into the District Bank in the 1920s. The manager lived 'above the shop'.

The Public Hall, Towngate, 1950. Outside the offices of the Leyland Urban District Council the barber, Booth Moss, in his white coat, has a word with Ben Pickup in his Triumph Mayflower, as a Fishwick's bus pulls out to pass.

Members of the LUDC outside the Public Hall,1937. Back row, left to right: councillors Lord, M.H.Wilkinson (Surveyor), Jackson, R.Armstrong (Clerk to the Council). Middle row: Marsden, Hocking, Parkinson, Hargreaves, Stansfield. Front row: Nelson, Lomax, Mrs Berry, Welsby, R.W.Lynn (clerk).

Leyland Urban District Council Fire Brigade, c.1910.

Leyland council's road roller, *c*.1920. A well-known sight, this engine did sterling work for many years on Leyland's roads.

Towngate cottages, *c*.1910. The three houses on the left were built on the site of a seventeenth century house. The Conservative club occupies a part of the site today.

Mrs Jolly's corner by the Ship Inn, *c*.1905. The sharp S-bend was the northernmost extent of the old linear village of Leyland.

Water Street, *c*.1900. Between Towngate and Hough Lane, Water Street was something of a hive of industry in the early nineteenth century as the old village began to expand northwards. The May Festival procession passes the weavers houses (right), and Sumners smithy (left).

Hough Lane, c.1905. In the years before the Great War Hough Lane was almost entirely residential. In 1905 Leyland Motors acquired land from Leyland Baldwin, which became the North Works. Later development on the opposite side of Hough Lane became the South Works.

Hough Lane, c.1959. The end of Wellington View, Lily Bank and Spring Bank, and the Congregational Church, later to become the United Reformed Church, with Brook Mill on the right.

A part of the Leyland Motors works on Hough Lane, *c.*1935. The South Works are top, and the North Works are bottom. From the air the scale of the industrial development of Hough Lane is very evident. The United Reformed Church is a prominent feature in the lower left, whilst the classic lines of the recently demolished Leyland Motors canteen building dominate the scene. A unique feature of this building was the reservoir which can clearly be seen on the roof. Now the town's shopping area, most of the frontage was still houses with gardens.

Hough Lane, c.1910.

Hough Lane shops, c.1916. Built as highly desirable residences, often with gardens in front, many houses were converted into shops to supply the needs of the enormous numbers of people travelling into the town daily, as Hough Lane became the hub of Leyland Motors.

Industrial Leyland, looking NE from the top of the Post Office, 1935. Leyland gasworks dominates the scene with the spectacular chimney of Farington Mill in the background.A good illustration of the new industrial Leyland which developed away from the old village centre around the cross.

Green's Hippodrome, Preston Road, *c*.1920. Leyland's first cinema.

Chapel Brow, c.1910.

Left: The Leyland and Farington Co-operative Society headquarters c.1905. Built in 1903, this shop contained the Co-ops non-food department. The upper stories housed the society's offices.

Below: Bread and confectionary delivery cart c.1910. A feature of the Co-op was the door to door service that it provided. It's milk floats, butchers vans, fruit and vegetable carts and coal deliveries, were all part of the day to day scene in Leyland and Farington.

Coal delivery, Golden Hill Terrace, c.1920.

Golden Hill Lane, c.1900. At the start of the twentieth century the seat of Leyland's rubber manufacturers still maintained a markedly rural aspect on the edge of the wetlands to the west.

A Fishwick's outing, c.1912. John Fishwick & Sons, one of a number of local carriers, expanded rapidly between the wars. This is an outing of staff from Leyland Motors. Back row, left to right: Evelyn Buckley, Tom Clarkson, Percy Barrow, Dick Sumner, -?-, -?-, Jim Bamber, -?-. Middle row: -?-, -?-, George Birtill, Bob Clayton, -?-, Bill Sumner, Bill Lowe, Jim Sumner, -?-, Alan Copley, Harry Horner, Sam Sutton, -?-, -?-. Front row: -?-, -?-, Bill Brown, Bill Valentine, -?-, -?-, -?-, -?-, Ralph Arrowsmith.

Turpin Green Lane, c.1920. The flag-stone walling around the gardens of these stone cottages was a local feature.

Five

South of Leyland Cross

The view from the cross looking down Worden Lane to Worden Park and Worden Hall, home of the Faringtons, the Lords of the Manor, c.1910.

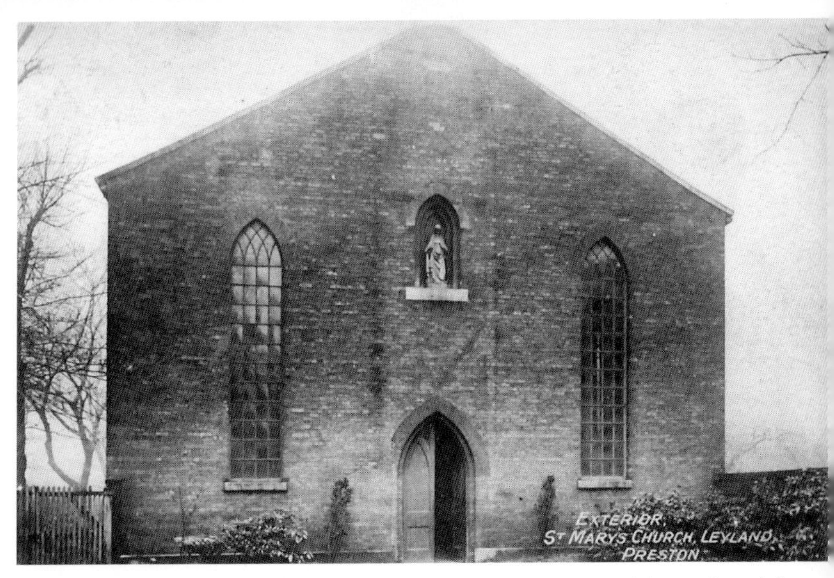

St Mary's RC church, Worden Lane, c.1910. Built in 1854, this church served the parish until the new church on Broadfield Drive was opened in 1964.

Clough House and cottage, c.1908. The impressive entrance to Worden Park can be seen in the distance.

The view from Clough House cottage, looking back to Leyland Cross, c.1905.

The vicarage, c.1930. Believed to be the site of the ancient vicarage of Leyland, this building stands behind Clough House and now forms a part of the church hall. The last occupant was Leyland Baldwin, who retired as vicar at the end of 1911. His successor built a new vicarage, now known as Chestnut Court.

Left: The new vicarage, seen from Worden Lane, 1937.

Below: The Vicar's Fields, *c*.1900. A popular walk for Leylanders in the past, these fields between Church Road and Worden Lane, are now extensively built over. The lower part of Park Road lies to the right, and Crocus Fields to the left.

The entrance to Worden Park, 1911.

Worden Hall from the south, c.1930. The home of the Faringtons, and formerly known as Shaw Hall.

Above: The front of the hall, with the sunken garden to the left, *c.*1910. The hall was abandoned after the fire of 1941, and after standing empty for many years was eventually demolished. Of this view only the greenhouses remain.

Left: William Edmund Farington (1886-1909), 1908. On the death of Susan Maria Farington – the last of the Faringtons of Worden – in 1894 the estate passed to a young boy, William Edmund, of the Isle of Wight branch of the family. When of age he married, and the young couple took up residence at the hall, amidst great celebrations in the village.

Mr and Mrs Farington outside the front of Worden Hall, 1908. He died in 1909, and his widow in 1910, whereupon the estate passed to the Wigan branch of the family. Henry Nowell Farington was squire at Leyland from 1910 until his death in 1947. The estate then passed to the present Sir Henry Farington of Somerset. Acquired by Leyland Urban Distruct Council, the park was opened to the public during the Festival of Britain celebrations in 1951.

The entrance hall, Worden, c.1905. The building was a treasure house of antiques, especially furniture and paintings.

The Gallery, Worden Hall, *c*.1905. The gallery, which fronted the sunken garden, was built by Sir William Farington in the mid-eighteenth century, to house his collection of classical antiques.

The Gallery, Worden Hall, *c*.1905.

Right: The Monument, Worden park, c.1905. Removed following the death of Henry Nowell Farington, the obelisk now stands before the parish church at Churchtown, near Southport.

Below: The North Lodge, Worden park, c.1905.

A panorama of the hall and sunken garden, *c.*1880. Apart from the wholesale removal of most of the house this view is surprisingly little changed today. The two elderly ladies in the small group to the left of the fountain, are Susan Maria Farington and her sister Mary Hannah.

The second park entrance, seen from Back Lane, now Langdale Road, *c*.1910. The Lodge which stood at these gates has subsequently been demolished.

Swiss Lodge, the third entrance to the park, *c*.1905.

The hall from across the park, seen from beside Altcar Farm, *c*.1905.

The Ice House, Worden Park, *c*.1905. The sculptures set into the front of this remarkable structure appear to have come from the ancient nave of the Parish church. The Ice House has recently been restored.

The Lodge in the park, c.1900. This building stood on the site now occupied by the public car park, off Worden Lane. It predated the formation of the park, being built in 1761 by a Captain Isaac Hamon of the Queens Royal Regiment, who had married the squire's sister.

Worden Hall in the 1950s. The top floor had been removed after the fire. Although the main body of the building has subsequently been demolished, the remaining outbuildings have been restored, and now house the thriving Worden Arts Centre.

Squire Farington (centre) with a group outside the south wing of the hall, c.1935. Henry Nowell Farington was the last of Leyland's squires. In 1941 he placed the enormous family and estate archives in the care of the Lancashire Record Office (now in Bow Lane, Preston), where they are freely available to the public. Following his death many of the house's contents were sold at auction, and the buildings and park were acquired by the local council.

The people of Leyland acquire Worden Park, as the mayor, Frank Marsden, opens the gates to the public during the Festival of Britain celebrations, 1951. An important consequence of this purchase, was to secure the park from housing development.

Six

East of Leyland Cross

Looking east from the cross, c.1905. The tower of St Andrew's parish church dominates Church Road.

St Andrew's church, 1920. In the foreground is the 'council yard', on which the town's War memorial was erected in 1929. The line of lime trees close to the north wall of the church became unsafe, and was removed in the 1930s.

St Andrew's church, 1910. The Old Grammar School is just visible through the arch at the top of Church Brow.

Above: The Old Grammar School, c.1920. Much of this building dates from about 1580, the school having been established in 1524. After 350 years the school closed in 1874. The schoolmaster's house to the right continued to be occupied, and the school itself served for many years as a church hall.

Right: Mr. Sumner, his wife and their grandson Peter c.1905. The Sumners occupied the master's house in the years up to the Great War. Peter and his friend Bill Rigby, long remembered the spectacular passage of Halley's Comet over Leyland in 1910, an event they observed from the pitch darkness of the adjacent churchyard.

The Old Grammar School, *c*.1950. Though occupied into the 1960s, the fabric of the buildings had deteriorated markedly by the late 1970s, when it was planned to demolish them to make way for a car-park. Acquired by South Ribble Borough Council for £1 and extensively restored, the buildings entered a new phase of their use as the Borough's Museum and Exhibition Centre in 1978. Among many other curiosities, Peter Sumner's initials can still be seen on the beam where he carved them in 1911. The Centre is open to the public, Tuesdays and Fridays 10 am to 1pm, Thursdays 1pm to 4 pm, and Saturdays 10am to 1 pm.

Procession passing the Old Grammar School, *c*.1913. Whitsuntide processions used to form up along this stretch of Church Road, close by the Eagle and Child Inn.

The Coronation Arch, Church Road, 1902.

Left: Church Road, *c*.1910. A view of the Eagle and Child and the Parish church, from the east. The stone barn which stood by the junction with Balcarres Road can be seen on the right, and the row of lime trees along the churchyard wall can be seen towering over the Old Grammar School.

Below: Church Road in the1930s. Lined by hedges with a canopy of trees, before the development of Stokes Hall on the right, and the building on the Mayfield on the left. The scene also provides a clue to Church Road's ancient origins as a sunken trackway worn by generations of worshippers from the Moor Quarter of the Parish.

The Maypole dance on the Mayfield, 1908. By 1900 the May Festival committee had rented the North Paddock on Church Road for the annual festival. The May Festival Ground was the start and finishing point for the procession and subsequent activities.

Wellington House, Church Road, c.1930. Built about the time of Waterloo, Wellington House was one of Leyland's largest houses. Rebuilt in 1861, after the first war it was acquired by Leyland Motors for use as a residence for premium apprentices. After Stokes Hall was built for this purpose, the house stood empty for many years before being demolished. The Masonic Hall was built on the site- renamed Wellington Park, in 1989.

Church Road, c.1910. The stone wall around the grounds of Wellington House can be seen on the left, and Beechfield Lodge stands on the right. The centre group comprises, left to right: Mrs Lord, Mr Lord, Mrs Baxendale and two children, Annie Lord and Matty Butcher.

Beechfield Lodge, c.1900. Beech Villa, as Beechfield was then known, was built in 1855 by John Morrell, the land agent to the Farington estate.

The Beechfield Rifle range, 1907. Built in 1906 behind Beechfield House, this was Leyland Rifle Club's first range. Ralph d'Albini Morrell can be seen examining the butts. Subsequently Captain Morrell of the Kings Own (Royal Lancaster Regiment), he was killed on the Somme on the 8th of August 1916.

Balshaws Grammar School,1931. Balshaws school was founded by Richard Balshaw in 1782, and two years later the first school was built on Golden Hill Lane. In 1904 a new school was added , but by the 1920s this also proved too small. A new site was obtained on Church Road and the present school opened in 1931.

New Inn, Wigan Road, *c*.1905. This fine three storey eighteenth-century house at the junction of Heald House Lane, Dawson Lane and the A49, was originally planned to replace 'Rose Whittles public house. Although it was accordingly called New Inn, there is no record of it ever having been a public house. A farm house, it was demolished when the Royal Ordnance Factory was built in the late 1930s.

Old Worden Hall, *c*.1895. This ancient corner of Leyland was the home of the Faringtons from the mid-sixteenth to the mid-eighteenth centuries. Located off Dawson Lane, and for half a century deep within the closed grounds of the Ordnance factory, much of the original timber work is intact, and the opportunity for its restoration in the near future is a real possibility.

Seven

West of Leyland Cross

The top of Fox Lane looking west from the Cross, c.1900.

Rag and bone man's assistant touting for trade in Union Street, *c*.1910.

Mr Weaver's class at St Andrews 'bottom school', 1914. Back row, left to right: Ditchfield, Gore, Rigby, Tattersall, Stephenson, Taylor, Gore, Parker. Front row: Stephenson, Taylor, Mr Weaver, Rigby, Hill.

Fox Lane c.1905. Fox Lane was formerly called Union Street at the Leyland Cross end, and Brook Street at the Seven Stars end. In between it was a country lane prior to the housebuilding of the 1930s and the years after the second world war.

Fox Lane Cricket Field 1904. Leyland Cricket Club was founded in 1848 and re-formed by John Stanning in 1862. Early opponents included the North End club, and Allen Hill, of Yorkshire and England, was the club's professional. He was the first man to take a wicket in a Test Match, and is buried at St Andrew's.

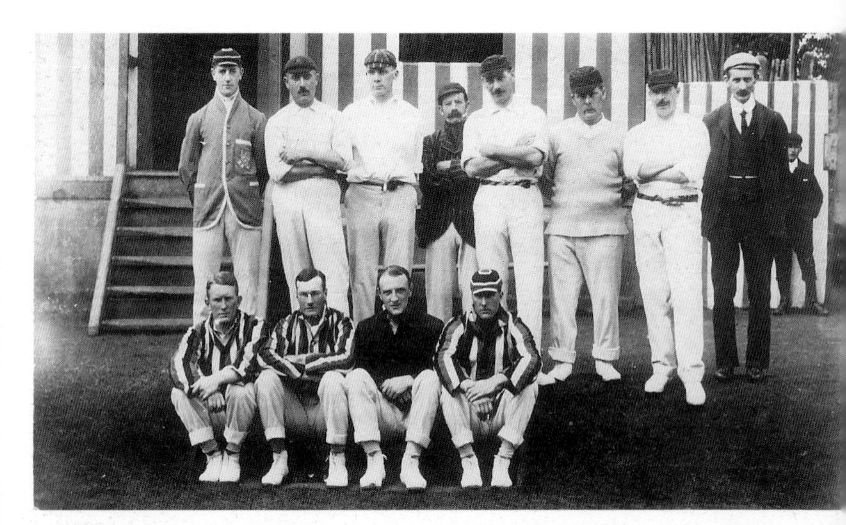

Leyland 1st Eleven 1906. Back row, left to right:: D.Brown, I'Anson, Turner, Tonge, Wilmot, Bennison, Cain, J.Hunt, (scorer), Front row: Messrs E.Stanning, J. Stanning, Walter Brearley, D.Stanning.

Leyland Rifle Club, Fox Lane, 1945. Back row, left to right:, Ray Goode, Eddie Grice, -?-, Eric Hirstle, -?-. Middle row: Jim Melling, Frank Preston, Guy Nicholson, Newton Iddon, John Mills, -?-. Front row: Charlie McHugh, Mr Butterworth, Bill Ratcliffe, -?-, -?-, Harry Waring, Capt.Bishop.

Squire Farington at a shoot, 1939. By tradition the Rifle Club's opening shoot of the season was begun by Squire Farington, here seen with Newton Iddon.

Seven Stars, with Mount Pleasant mill in the distance, 1920. The setts, or cobbles, in the road here are interesting. Very few roads in Leyland had them, but this part of Leyland Lane was badly cut up by the wagons from Stannings Bleachworks on their way to and from Liverpool docks.

The Original Seven Stars, *c*.1920. Built in 1683 as a gentleman's residence, this building has been a public house since the 1880s, but there is some evidence that it was an Alehouse for a period in the mid- eighteenth century.

Seven Stars and Mount Pleasant Mill c.1930. To the right Slater Lane and Dunkirk Lane lead onto the Moss-Side.

Alma Cottages, *c*.1910. Standing opposite Mount Pleasant Mill, these millworkers cottages took their name from the Battle of the Alma during the Crimean War.

Mid-Leyland Lane, with Cowling Lane in the distance, *c*.1910. The bearded figure on the right appears on many Leyland photographs of the period. Who he was, or why he appears, is a mystery. Corrugated iron roofs, of the type on the very old cottage to the right, were often put over worn thatched roofs. When surviving examples are removed, the old thatch is frequently found intact beneath.

The mill dam, Mill Lane, Seven Stars, c.1950. The manorial mill fed by this mill dam and pool, occurs in records as early as 1250, as 'the Great Mill dam of Adam of Walton'. The water came from the springs and brooks that rise in the vicinity of Water Street.

Seven Stars looking south from the tower of Mount Pleasant Mill, c.1910.

The Seven Stars Hotel, *c.*1920. The 'Crofters' public house, seen further along Leyland Lane, took its name from a process at the Bleachworks, many of whose workers lived at Seven Stars.

In a Leyland Garden, *c.*1920.

Dunkirk Lane, c.1905. Originating as a track leading onto the mosses west of Leyland, this district has been extensively built over since the 1970s. From late medieval times Leyland began to encroach onto the moss-side west of Leyland Lane. The 'Long Meaniegate', mentioned in 1726, was constructed around the edge of the early enclosures and turf diggings or 'moss-rooms'.

St James's church Walking Day at Seven Stars, c.1908.

Slater Lane, c.1910. With the River Lostock in the foreground and St James's church in the distance, Leyland's western by-pass now cuts through this moss-land scene. Located on the edge of the moss, the church occupies an altogether different landscape from St Andrew's, though it lies only a mile to the west.

Slater Lane bridge, c.1910.

St James's church and cottage, *c*.1905. The cottage occurs on the earliest map of Leyland (1725). St James junior school now occupies the site.

Mr. William Waddicar standing outside his cottage, Slater Lane, *c*.1900. This close up of the cottage next to St James church, is a good illustration of the vernacular style of the district, using building materials which lay close to hand.

St James's vicarage, 1910. Now demolished, the vicarage stood behind the site of the present St James's Junior School.

The Revd C.E. Fynes-Clinton, vicar 1901-1921, with his family in the vicarage garden, c.1910.

A typical cottage on the edge of the moss, *c.*1910.

St James's school, Moss-side, *c.*1900. Founded by Samuel Crook in 1770, this building was built by the misses Farington in 1856.

Above: The Roundhouse on Leyland Moss c.1900. The last (or first) building in Leyland, located at the centre of the moss. Perhaps originating as a place for the collection of tolls on the Sod Hall Meanygate connecting Leyland to Longton, this unique and delightful structure was inhabited as late as 1982. Today only traces of the structure remain. Around it spread the extensive reclaimed mosslands which today form some of the most fertile soils in Lancashire, and give little indication of the fenlands which originally surrounded the Roundhouse.

Left: The Roundhouse, c.1920.

Eight

Leyland at War

Leyland men of the 'King's Liverpools' in camp, Salisbury Plain, 1915. Second from left: H.Langton, 3rd W.Cocker, 4th L.Cornwall, 6th N.Bannister. Over 250 Leyland men lost their lives in the Great War.

'Royal Flying Corps type' wagon, in service in Arras, France, 1918. Leyland Motors produced almost 6,000 vehicles for the War Office between August 1914 and the Armistice, the great majority of them for the RFC, which subsequently became the RAF. The two world wars were to be an important stimulus to the company, leading to enormous expansion of productive capacity at Leyland.

Unveiling of the Leyland War Memorial, Church Road, 9th November 1929. The ceremony was performed by Major W.Jervoise Collas of Preston, and Mr Charles Porter of Leyland, who was blinded in the war. The dedication was performed by the Bishop of Whalley.

The Local Defence Volunteer Corps, 'A' and 'C' Platoon, Runshaw Hall, July 1940. The forerunner of the Home Guard.

Remembrance Day parade, November 1940. 'B' Company Leyland Home Guard on Chapel Brow. Captain Pease and Lt. Jump lead up the men.

Officers of 'B' Company, 12th County of Lancaster (Leyland) Battalion Home Guard, 1944. Back row, left to right: Lt. Collard, Lt. Boyce, Lt. Lewis, Lt. Goode, Lt. Samuels, Lt. Nicholson, Lt. Waterhouse, Lt. Beardsworth, Lt. Castle, Lt. Fallon. Middle row: Lt. Bolton, Lt. Jones, Lt. Postlethwaite, Lt. Barrand, Lt. Morris, Lt. Hirstle, Lt. Sandham, Lt. Price. Front row: Lt. Mills, Capt. Cank (MO), Capt. Bishop, Maj. Waring, Capt. Melling, Capt. Birtill, Lt. Norris.

HMS *Marguerite*, 1940. The corvette was adopted by Leyland in 1942, and the commemorative plaque from the ship is preserved in the museum. Large sums of money were raised for the war effort in annual war savings weeks. 'Warship Week' in 1942 raised £148,322, and the 'Wings for Victory' campaign the following year achieved £176,315 – a very large sum for a town of less than 15,000 people.

Leyland Comet tanks moving deep into Hitler's Reich, March 1945. The number of men employed at Leyland Motors increased by nearly half to 9,000, and the number of women rose from under 500 in 1939 to almost 3,000 in 1944. Output during these years has been described as, 'Tanks and more tanks'. The King and Queen visited the factories in November 1941.

Archbishop Downey's visit to the forces canteen at Leyland Cross, 1943. Back row: 2nd left Edgar Trevett, 3rd left Mrs Barrow. Front row: 4th left Fr. Lightbound, 6th left, Mrs Farrelly.

The stand down of 'B' Company, Leyland Home Guard, 3 December 1944. After marching around Leyland the parade re-formed on Worden Park. Major Waring, OC 'B' Company, addressed the men, and thanked them for their loyalty and support. Many of the men had served throughout the war.

Left: An unexploded bomb, dropped on Leyland Motors, 1940. The motor works, and the enormous Royal Ordnance Factory at Euxton, were targets of the enemy's air war. Locals were addressed directly by William Joyce, 'People of Leyland...Yooks-Ton is burning!', and Leyland Motors's Farington works was attacked on a number of occasions. On Monday 21 October 1940 one bomb hit the Axle factory, a second the Tank factory, and a third destroyed the Foundry roof. A raid six days later missed the works, but hit Ward Street, Lostock Hall, killing twenty four people. Bombs dropped on the 30th of October hit their targets but failed to explode.

Below: The River Lostock, Leyland, 1947. A post-war use was found for the concrete tank-traps which were such a common feature of war-time Britain. Here they are used to counter the effects of erosion on the banks of the river.

The New Leyland; Broadfield Drive, 1948. Started in 1945, with the help of Italian prisoner of war labour, the Broadfield Estate was Leyland Urban District Council's first large scale post-war building project. When completed it covered the whole area bounded by the Cross, Seven Stars, Earnshaw Bridge and Golden Hill.

The opening of the Council's first Broadfield houses, on Saturday 24 January 1948. The Chairman of the Council, Mr James Tomlinson hands over the keys to Mr and Mrs Weller. Left to right: Councillors Welsby, Frank Howe (Surveyor), Andrew Tomlinson (builder), Nelson, Tomlinson, Marsden, Parkinson, Mr and Mrs Weller, Oliver, Dr Fotheringham, and Mrs Kelley.

The Festival of Britain Celebrations, Worden Lane, 1951. The 1951 celebrations were probably the most extensive and significant in the town's history, and were marked by great optimism for the future. Here the procession is being filmed for later showing at a local cinema. The film is preserved in the North West Film Archive.

The Festival Queen, Jean Lawrence, and her attendants, on newly opened Worden Park, 1951. Deepdale worthies entertain the crowds on Worden Park,1951. Jean Lawrence, with Mr and Mrs Marsden, and North End's Jimmy Milne, Tommy Finney, Joe Marston and Willie Cunningham.

Climbing the greasy pole, Festival of Britain celebrations, Worden Park, 1951. Leylanders enter the second half of the twentieth century.

A popular Leyland Postcard of the 1920s.

Acknowledgements

The photographs in this book are largely drawn from South Ribble's local history collection housed at the Museum and Exhibition Centre in Church Road, Leyland. Important collections include those assembled, throughout their life-times, by William Rigby, William Dawber, Bert Morris and Charles Lockwood. Both the museum and the authors, are grateful to acknowledge the kind donation of the items used in this book, by Mr Rigby, Miss Lockwood, Mr Platt, Mr Berry, Mr Houghton, Mrs Baxter, Miss Whitehead, Mrs Chamberlain, Mr and Mrs Iddon, Col. Worden (Vermont, USA), Mrs Hudson, Miss Buckley, Mrs Casey, Mrs Logan, Mrs Watkinson, Leyland UDC, and Mr Damp. A great number of people have assisted in many ways, by loaning additional photographs, helping to identify scenes and clarifying details. A great debt is accordingly owed to Les Southworth, Gwen Buckley, William Preston, Gladys Thomas, Beryl Caunce, Dr Fotheringham, Elizabeth Shorrock, Ron Berry, Eveline Hewitt, Robert Harrison, Harry Ashurst, Valerie Kite and Anne Hunt. The Leyland Historical Society, Mrs Penman, Mrs Kazer, Mr Waring and Mr Southworth kindly loaned photographs to fill existing gaps in the museum's collection. A number of the photographs of the Leyland and Birmingham Rubber Co. are reproduced by the kind consent of the Lancashire County Library Service. Particular thanks are due to Francis Turner, Dr Rex Pope of the University of Central Lancashire, the Friends of the Museum, Robert Rushton and the staff of Leyland Library, and to Dave Lewis of the Leyland Photographic Society for his advice on the selection of photographs.